Spirituality Should be Divorced from Religion

By the Reverend George Tarleton

London | New York

Published by Clink Street Publishing 2018

Copyright © 2018

First edition.

The author asserts the moral right under the Copyright, Designs and Patents Act 1988 to be identified as the author of this work.

All rights reserved. No part of this publication may be reproduced, stored in a retrieval system or transmitted, in any form or by any means without the prior consent of the author, nor be otherwise circulated in any form of binding or cover other than that with which it is published and without a similar condition being imposed on the subsequent purchaser.

ISBN:
978-1-912850-40-2 - paperback
978-1-912850-41-9- ebook

Surely spiritualty and religion are the same? No they are fundamentally different – one is a bird in a cage and the other a bird on the wing. All religions have their own individual cages with their different beliefs and different gods. As there are now more than 200 religious deities, we usually opt for the one that our parents worshiped. I was a minister of the Christian religion for the first half of my working life and a businessman for the second half when I enjoyed the luxury of spiritual freedom.

I am using the word 'reverend' because I was never officially 'unfrocked', as the man who ordained me, Dr Martyn Lloyd Jones, had died before I quit. My wife's brother, who is also a minister, wasn't happy with the situation so he drove down from Manchester to the New Forest in his best suit to unfrock me. When my wife found out what he intended to do, she kicked him out of our cottage before he could do anything. She has never done that to anyone in all the 60 years of our married life. I found it very difficult to stop bursting out laughing. So I am still a 'reverend' but this is last time I shall ever use it.*

Having experienced both ways of living I have come to the conclusion that spirituality flourishes much better outside the cages of religion. Christianity, for example, controls the way we think and act from some dusty manuscripts that they claim are the words of God with nothing to back up their claim.

The Ten Commandments were introduced by Moses who was an African born in Egypt. He was familiar with the ten categories of sin which existed in that country along with the unique concept of monotheism which the Pharaoh had just introduced in Egypt. So the Ten Commandments are African in origin.

There are 66 books in the Bible written by 40 different authors over a period of 1500 years which Christians claim

---

* When I left I wrote *Birth of a Christian Anarchist* and started with the words 'MENE MENE TEKEL UPARSIN' which is the writing on the wall that dramatically appeared at Belshazzar's Feast. It marked the end of his reign. My aim was to apply it to the end of Christianity but now I realise that it applies to all religion which is beginning to lose its weird grip on mankind.

Spirituality Should be Divorced from Religion

were inspired by God and are 'without error'. It seems to have taken God a long time to make up his mind... Despite studying theology at college and fooling the university that I understood what I read, I have to confess that I was confused.

Some people got hold of my book's launch tape and started a website called 'Whatever Happened to George Tarleton?' to have a go at me and prove their belief in fundamentalism which is no fun, all mental and full of -isms. There are now hundreds of individual fundamentalist sects who claim only their unique interpretation of the Bible is the correct one!

When I came across this site years ago, I decided not to respond as people would forget me in time. They didn't. The people who wrote about me never knew me but realised that I used to believe the Bible was the word of God. It is difficult to explain how reasonably intelligent people like me could accept this incredible claim, but I did.

However the New Testament wasn't believed to be God's word during the first three centuries. Then, every book was held by some to be sacred and by others to be a forgery. The Old Testament was rightly described by the apostle Paul as 'crap'. The reason for these original different opinions is that truth cannot be contained in the beautiful pages of the Bible. Truth is a bird on the wing and cannot be confined – which is why it sets us free.

I no longer have faith in faith but prefer what Life has taught me because Life is the great teacher. 'It is a far worthier thing to read by the light of experience than to adorn yourself with the labours of others,' said Leonardo Da Vinci.

Our basic problem stems from not knowing who we really are. We derive our false sense of who we are from our race, religion and roles in life. Ultimately they are just thoughts precariously held together by the fact that our whole sense of self is invested in them. Believers are defined by someone else's belief. However when you have experience you don't have to believe because you know and are not at the mercy of someone who merely has an argument.

Sit down and watch the moments unfold with no agenda other than to be fully present. Every time the mind wanders bring it back to the breath in all its vividness. Being aware of just your breathing not only takes you away from thinking, it also creates an inner silence which allows your sensory perception to be sharper and more intense. Whenever you are only conscious of your breath you are absolutely present.

This way of living is a pathless path that is not revealed by ideas because it is beyond concepts. It happens when we are transported into another realm, where the spirit soars beyond the boundaries of ordinary perception. This opens up the vast free spirit within us. It is a release from the confines of the mind into the cosmic orgasm of the Universe

Before writing my new book, I decided to check on how *Christian Anarchist* was doing. I was shocked at first to find second-hand copies being sold for £100 when the original cost was just a few quid, and felt I was to blame. Over time the price went up to £500. A friend of mine has just returned from America where it is being sold for £1000! When I initially came across these ridiculous prices I thought that I had become famous in my 25 year absence. Sadly I have just discovered it was just a money laundering scam which the police are now investigating.

I feel partly responsible for this situation as I didn't take any interest in the sale of my book. The reason was that I was starting my new business as a hearing aid audiologist in the private sector. This took up all my time and I had no energy for anything else. Having read my book after 25 years I was surprised at my reaction – I enjoyed it. This has prompted me to reproduce the original book which cost me £1000, and I will sell it on Amazon for £6.99. If you want to know about my religious past that is the place to start.

In the Beginning

The majesty and mystery of the Universe provokes a sense of awe that none of the gods made in our image can match. In the beginning, before the Universe existed, scientists claim that everything that was or will be was condensed into a tiny speck they call a 'singularity'. Then the Big Bang occurred – a term used by one of its opponents in jest at the time. The term Big Bang describes what happened within less than a second when entire Universe was born!

Where did this 'singularity' come from? 'There is absolutely no way to tell what made it happen,' says Stephen Hawking, who has just died. Genesis, with its simple six day creation, presents a theological explanation but doesn't claim to be historical. Both accounts need faith to accept their version. Gravity, not god, is the great creator of the Universe, for it created order out of the original chaos in our dynamic and turbulent Universe.

The Universe is not just stranger than we imagine – it is stranger than we can imagine. The curvature of space-time is a theory which Einstein first proposed, about a mysterious force which warps space and time. The concept that time and the three-dimensional are fused into a four-dimensional continuum is now accepted by scientists. Space and time aren't different in any fundamental way, however combining the two helps cosmologists understand how the Universe works at the big level of galaxies and the small level of atoms.

George Tarleton

Truth is that which Cannot be Expressed

When I was first introduced to Malcolm Muggeridge I was delighted to meet one of the great journalists of the twentieth century. He had interviewed Hitler, Mussolini and Stalin and said they all lacked one thing: a sense of humour – especially about themselves.

I was also impressed when we were having a private conversation and I challenged him saying, 'Malcolm you are ignoring the facts.' His reply stunned me. 'There are no such things as facts, dear boy,' said the famous journalist. 'Life is a drama and we all see it from our own perspective.' What a profound insight from one of a great observer of mankind. Certainty divides us, but doubt unites us as we all have a unique experience of life. Agreeing to disagree makes life more interesting.

Living without religious beliefs, as I do now, means I don't have to interpret Life through the dull light of some clever person's dogma. One of the great Chinese mystics said 'Truth is that which cannot be expressed.' It is so vast that the moment you try define it you lose the length, breadth, depth and height of its scope.

God is not found in any of the religious structures of the world but within us for we are divine in our deepest identity. Which one of the 200 gods does that refer to? None of them! They are all too small to define the One who is everywhere. When we eventually emerge from our small ideas of divinity, we begin to see an awesome being who is not a thing but the mysterious everything.

Do I miss preaching? No, because preaching is the art of dividing people into sheep who agree with them and goats who don't – and I am now clearly on the side of the goats. However I have to admit that one of the highlights of my life was when I preached to over 6000 people in the Albert Hall.

At the time I still believed that the Bible was the final authority. So I showed that there are only three kinds of church

Spirituality Should be Divorced from Religion

in the New Testament: the church in the house, the church in an area like Corinth and the universal church. I ended by saying that 'denominations are an abomination as they dissected Christ's body with their petty doctrinal differences.' This made the headlines in the religious press.

Religion has created a world that only the ordained leaders can control. So we created something over which religious leaders had no control: 'The House Church Movement'. Sadly it no longer exists as it has drifted back into its old evangelical fold. I foresaw this eventuality when I was last allowed to express my doubts publicly about the movement I was involved in. What I did not realise at the time was that this was to be my final public appearance ever – even though the young people were on their feet applauding me at the end.

Preachers are there to dispel to doubt. They see life as a problem they have solved, whereas life is a mystery to be experienced. Preachers perpetuate the nonchalant lie that their message is the answer to the profound mystery of Life. However if we go deep inside – past the clutter of everyday consciousness – we then discover who we really are.

Doctor Yuval Noah Harari, the author of *Sapiens: A Brief History of Humankind* had a remarkable effect on my thinking. The conclusions I had come to about religion are the same as his about the world in general. He says 'There are no gods in the universe, no nations, no money, no human rights outside the common imaginations of human beings. Unlike lying, an imagined reality is something that everyone believes in and, as long as the communal belief persists, the imagined reality exerts force in the world.'

John Lennon's 'Imagine' was released in 1971. It is one of the most beautiful and awe-inspiring songs of all time encouraging us to use our collective imagination. 'Imagine there's no heaven – it's easy if you try. Nothing to live or die for and no religion too.' He was a modern day prophet and I want that song to be sung at my funeral which is getting closer as I have just completed my eightieth orbit of the sun.

George Harrison wrote 'My Sweet Lord' the year before Lennon wrote 'Imagine'. It topped the charts worldwide. However I felt he had chosen the wrong lord (Hare Krishna) and rather arrogantly decided to tell him so. When I arrived at the gates of Harrison's vast mansion and strolled in, a large dog came barking up to me. Not knowing what to do I asked him to take me to his master; he didn't because his master was in Bangladesh at the time. However the dog led me to his mother-in-law who was sunbathing in the garden. So I told her about my mission to change George's mind.

I would never have succeeded with changing George's mind but I did in converting her. I now regret the large number of people I converted to Christianity, but there is nothing I can do about it now except to explain my simplistic approach to the Bible.

Also hearing Billy Graham preach his simple message with such conviction at his first crusade in England was a defining moment in my life. Much later I became part of Graham's team for 'Spree 73' and preached about the dangers of the dangers of the occult to thousands of people. As a result my book *The Occult Mushroom* became an instant best seller.

The Dangers of the Occult

'Why don't you fuck off' shouted a well-dressed elderly lady. As I was in the middle of giving my lecture on the dangers of getting involved in the occult in a packed Anglican church, I didn't take any notice of her. So she got up out of her pew to eject me! It took her husband and a couple of strong men to stop her and bundle her into the vestry. When she had calmed down, I found out that she had been involved in witchcraft. So I released her from its power.

A year later I received a letter from her saying her friend had just told her what she had said to me. She was horrified and asked me to forgive her. I said there was nothing to forgive as she was being controlled by the power she had allowed into her life when she was younger. What we fail to realise is that witchcraft is a religion and whatever religion we subscribe to, we are submitting to their spiritual authority.

While that is understandable with witchcraft, what about just playing with the Ouija board, isn't it just for a bit of fun as many people think when they dabble with it on Halloween? Just to help out at my local school I offered to teach a class of drop-outs who were just filling time until they left school. 'What do you think of the Ouija board game?' I asked. The rogue of the class said 'We think it is evil!' I didn't think the word existed in his limited vocabulary.

When I asked him to explain he said: 'We were playing with an upturned glass and the letters of the alphabet surrounding it. When we asked it questions, we felt one of us was moving it so we asked it to break Joe Blogs' leg. The glass shattered and we were shocked. Then we heard an ambulance entering the school grounds and fund out that Blogs had fallen down stairs and broken his leg.' The whole class confirmed his story.

It was nearly midnight when the phone rang. 'We have a boy in hospital who has been in a trance state for three whole days. Can you help?' said the policeman. A few minutes later I was bombing up the road to Whips Cross Hospital in a police car. The boy was lying on a bed in casualty with his hands crossed on his chest, staring vacantly at the ceiling.

When I asked where the father was, they told me he wouldn't come near the boy because he had been so violent. This happened when they brought the boy to the hospital and tried to keep him there by force. 'He went berserk, clawed his brother to the ground and ran off into the night.'

When the police caught up with him, he claimed to be Moses at first and then Jesus Christ. When I asked his father how this all began he said 'It all started when my son and his friends at the Tech College were playing Ouija.' So I ordered the spirit of the glass to leave him. Within ten minutes he had returned to normal, much to the amazement of all. This seemingly innocent game can have strange consequences and my advice about playing with the Ouija board is DON'T!

There is a religious sect that only allows husband and wife to have sex through the hole in the bed sheet that the sect demands must divide them. It is presumably their idea of holiness? What an insane way to stop people doing what comes naturally, but that is what religion does especially when it comes to sex.

When I use the words 'bondage of religion' I am using the word 'bondage' as a sadomasochistic sexual practice. It is when a man asks a woman to abuse him sexually and then pays her for doing it! Religion also makes you suffer sexually and expects you to pay financially for it by supporting religion

When I asked Dr Andrew Walker to write a description of me he said 'George Tarleton is always breaking free and running to the light.' That is the most succinct description of my character you will ever find. I have broken free from the bondage of religion and now run toward the light of Life.

Spirituality is to do with living now and experiencing eternity now while you are still alive. Dying is not the only way out of time – you can move out of time and experience eternity now. Past and future are just concepts we have invented to create a context for our present experience. Your inner body is like wormhole in the space-time continuum which leads from the here and now to the always and everywhere. Your body is not an obstacle to a free spirit but a springboard from which the spirit can take flight.

George Tarleton

The Jesus Story

When I went to my first carol service in over thirty years, a line in Charles Wesley's beautiful carol 'Hark the Herald Angels Sing' which says 'late in time behold him come' started me thinking. Why did God wait for 3000 years of civilisation to elapse before sending his son to die a gruesome death on the cross? Why couldn't he just forgive humanity for not obeying his laws which only the Jews knew? Why send him to a backwater like Jerusalem rather than Rome which was the centre of the world?

He would have got a better reception in Egypt where the earliest religious text tell of a god called Osiris became flesh. He wandered through Egypt teaching people how to live. He was finally put to death by the forces of evil but restored magically to life and ascended to heaven to become the judge of souls in the afterlife. Sound familiar?

Over the next 2000 years, before the supposed birth of Jesus on the 25th of December – the birthday of the Sun God – cultures around the Mediterranean adopted this strange Egyptian myth and made it their own. When the mystery schools died out in the first century, Gnostics took the myth over from them. Jewish Gnostics then created an allegorical story portraying their messiah as the hero of a mystery religion. In their hands the genocidal messiah of Judaism (Joshua) is born again as the gentle Jesus, which is Joshua's name in Greek.

This Joshua/Jesus was then transformed from a xenophobic Jew who conquers his enemies with extreme violence into a pacifist advocating non-violence. Instead of demanding the Old Testament's eye for an eye, this new Joshua says you should love your enemies, which is what Socrates taught. Their Joshua/Jesus comes to bring personal not national salvation because their God is not a racist who only loves Jews but a father who loves all mankind. I have always thought it odd of God to choose the Jews.

The theologian Rudolph Bultmann devoted his whole life to studying the gospels. He concluded that in them there is

Spirituality Should be Divorced from Religion

'almost nothing concerning the life and personality of Jesus since the early Christians showed no interest in either.' That is because the Gospel story is not based on facts but on the Gnostic version of the pagan myth of the death and resurrection of the god-man.

Paul's letters, writings which are the earliest we have, do not contain a quasi-historical narrative about Jesus. His Christ is clearly a mystical figure who does not inhabit any particular time or place – he never quotes Jesus. His Christ is a mystical person whose story illuminates the path of mystical death and resurrection that his Gnostic readers need to follow if they want to experience the Christ within.

Over a century after Paul wrote his letters, four anonymous gospels appear. Later they are attributed to Matthew, Mark, Luke and John to give them the status of 'eyewitnesses'. The first three gospels appear to agree, mainly because they pinch a lot of Marks material.

Around the same time as these gospels appeared, Justin (who was rejected by both the Pythagorean and Platonic mystery schools) set up his own Christian cult. In an overcrowded spiritual market place, Christianity was just a fringe sect competing for adherents. So Justin claimed that the god-man of the mystery schools was just a myth, but his god-man 'Jesus' came in the flesh and lived them out.

He was the first to claim that the Jewish messiah and the gentile god-man had incarnated in one man in one place at one time. This was revolutionary and the Christian sect began to grow from that point onward. While I do not accept that the gospels are based on facts, I accept they tell the greatest story ever told – but it is still just a story.

The Roman Church

Although the Romans kept detailed records, strangely no account of the trial and execution of Jesus have ever been found. The most famous Jewish historian, Josephus, wrote a history of the Jews in great detail. He would have been a contemporary of Jesus but appears to dismiss him in a paragraph. However, once this obvious interpolation is removed, the text flows more easily and makes more sense. It is now believed to have been inserted when Christianity was made the official religion of the Roman Empire.

The Emperor Constantine was supposed to have been converted to Christianity – but he was only baptised on his deathbed. This sun-worshipping soldier was obviously keeping all his options open until the very last possible moment. What attracted Constantine to Christianity was not its doctrine but that he could adapt it to suit his authoritarian nature.

He found the church was divided over the nature of Jesus with some claiming that he was just a man with wit and wisdom, while others claimed he was God made flesh. The emperor couldn't see the problem here, as some of the Roman emperors were declared as divine only after they died. So with his strong leadership this and many other doctrines were settled at the Council of Nicaea, which he convened. With the threat of banishment or death hanging over their heads, the bishops didn't dare disagree.

The civil war that bedevilled Christianity in the third and fourth centuries violently supressed the original Christians and branded them as heretics. The Roman Church won and spent the next 16 centuries systematically destroying all the evidence that this creative Christianity ever existed. That changed with the find of the Gnostic gospels in 1945 at Nag Hammadi in Egypt. They were buried around the third century and are evidence of that persecution.

The Gospel of Thomas was found there. It had 50 parallel sayings with Mark's Gospel but without any narrative at all. In

Spirituality Should be Divorced from Religion

this alternative gospel we encounter a Jesus with the wit of a cynic philosopher and the shock tactics of a zen master. As no dogmas could be founded on these pithy sayings, they were burned, but this one survived.

History is written by the winners. The Roman Church won and wrote their own account of the origins of Christianity, dismissing the original Christians as a cult of obscure heretics. From the beginning of the third century, with the backing of the Holy Roman Empire, Christians set about persecuting the gnostic and pagan religions out of existence with an unholy violence.

This unholy alliance between church and state did more than try to eradicate the popular religions – it began to destroy civilisation itself. Black robed monks destroyed the ancient historical treasures of pagan temples. Their priests and priestesses were murdered or exiled and the wealth of the temples shared out between the emperor and his bishops.

Constantine was a control freak which helped him become the greatest commander of the Roman army in history. He is matched in history only by that other truly great general Mohammed, who started Islam, which means 'surrender'. Both religions now top the religious charts with Christianity having over two billion members and Islam just under two billion. No wonder the religious deities they produced sound like these tyrannical despots who created them. All the religions of the world were created by control freaks and are maintained today by control freaks.

The saddest example of the Roman Church's control over its followers was when the AIDS virus first appeared in South Africa. The only way in which it could be controlled (before a cure was found) was by wearing a condom. Inexplicably the Church decreed that they must not be used as they encourage people to have sex. So thousands of people died because of the stupid ban and I find that is what the Roman Church calls 'an unforgivable sin'.

The Church's general attitude to sex is weird. The apostle Paul said 'it is better to marry than to burn' but to keep their priests pure, the Roman Church does not allow them to marry. So they burn and bugger up the lives of young boys who they are responsible for. To deny sex is futile, as it causes more problems than it solves. Sex is the most natural expression of our humanity and it is stupid to deny men and women enjoying it.

Turn your awareness inside yourself and hand over the control from your mind to your body for a change. Relying on instinct, move through the world with all the sense doors flung open. Look for a passionate expression of life that devours its delights. The sensation of pleasure when we connect with the wonders of life is biologically experienced through the effects of endorphins. They reduce tension, create physical feelings of wellbeing, euphoria and bliss states.

Endorphins are chemically similar to opium but are not addictive or damaging. They work toward healing wounded or damaged tissues and boost the immune system. Endorphins are responsible for the euphoria of athletes and the pleasure of sex.

Your Body

How did the primal soup of amino acids and other simple molecules manage to turn themselves into the first living cell some four billion years ago? The odds against this happening randomly are ridiculous. The unbelievable complexity of arrangement needed to produce life shows that intelligence must have been involved. But whose?

The extraordinary complicated creature that we are begins life as a tiny speck of DNA sitting in the middle of a fertilised egg. Research into DNA shows the unbelievable complexity of arrangements which are necessary to produce life. Sitting in the middle of every cell in your body off stage, DNA choreographs all that happens on stage.

Everything we do – think, speak, run or play a violin – builds on the capacity programmed into that original module. Each cell of the body contains all of the DNA's infinite possibilities all of the time. DNA is the source of all the proteins that repair cells, build new ones and replace missing or defective pieces of the genetic code.

The miracle of DNA is that it can turn so many abstract messages into life itself. What makes DNA mysterious is that it lives at the point of transformation and spends its whole life making more life. Also DNA does not just work from rote memory and can invent new chemicals at will. Exactly how this is done no one knows. Only 1% of the genetic material is used for all these complicates tasks. This leaves 99% doing things that science cannot account for.

We evolved from the from the great apes in Africa two million years ago and remained weak and marginal creatures for almost all those two million years until we learned to start fires and cook 300,000 years ago. Then we became the dominant species and ultimately the ape men became spacemen.

The human body is a single energy phenomenon. At one end the human body is experienced as the sex drive, at the other end it is experienced as ecstasy. As William Blake wrote 'Energy is eternal delight.' The energy of sex is divine as it is the source of the greatest miracle of all: the creation of life. Our bodies are the highest evolution of all life forms.

Your body is not an obstacle to a free spirit but the springboard from which our spirit can take flight. The early Eastern mystics are said to have gained their first glimpses of spiritual enlightenment at the moment of orgasm. Ecstasy implies that you are filled with emotions too powerful for the body to contain or the rational mind to understand. This opens up the vast free spirit inside your being.

We need to learn to mobilise our energy up through the energy centres in our body and experience it more fully. Our desire to unite sexually with another human being is a reflection of an underlying need to experience wholeness and complete intimacy which transcends the individual's sense of isolation and separateness.

'Suddenly the boundaries between our bodies dissolved and with it the distinction between man and woman. We were one. The experience became timeless, we were in ecstasy,' says Margot Anand in her book *The Art of Sexual Ecstasy*.

There are seven energy centres in the human body called 'chakras', from the Sanskrit word meaning 'wheel' as they are circular in shape: a whirling wheel of energy where matter and consciousness meet. This invisible energy is vital to the life force which keeps us vibrant and healthy. It is the place where body, mind and spirit are ultimately connected.

The first chakra gives us a sense of security and stability.

The second chakra is our sexual centre and source of our creativity.

The third chakra is the source our personal power.

The fourth chakra is the heart and the source of love and connection.

The fifth chakra is in throat and is the source of verbal expression and the ability to speak the highest truth.

The sixth chakra is called the third eye as it is located between the eyebrows and is the source of intuition.

The seventh chakra is in the crown of the head and gives enlightenment and spiritual connection to our higher selves.

The Mind

What is the mind? Is it just a complicated information processing device? Is it a person's ability to reason? Or is the mind a cognitive facility including perception, thinking, judgement and memory? Defining the mind is not easy as there is no single, agreed upon definition.

'The human mind is not capable of grasping the Universe,' said Einstein, one of the greatest minds ever. 'We are like little children entering a huge library. The walls are covered to the celling with books in many different tongues and the child knows that someone must have written these books. It does not know who or how and does not understand the language in which they were written. But the child notes a definite plan in the arrangements of these books. A mysterious order which it does not comprehend but only dimly suspects.'

Believing you are your mind is a delusion. 'I think therefore I am,' wrote Rene Descartes, the father of modern philosophy. However, identification with just the mind is an obstacle to experiencing who you truly are. Most people are completely identified with the noisy, incessant voice in their head even though most of its compulsive thinking is repetitive and often pointless. It is as though an entity has taken possession of them they are completely unaware of.

People ask me how I now explain the many healings I experienced if they were not the work of God. My answer is simple: it is all down to the power of positive thinking. The placebo effect is now a well-known psychological phenomenon. It is where a person improves after taking a chalk tablet simply because they believe that it will actually make them better.

With my being an ordained minister of religion at the time and quoting 'God's Word', it worked in one out of ten cases. For me it also explains why the majority of my exorcisms were successful as I then believed that evil spirits had no place in our body. I also believe that the power of negative thinking is very damaging and should be avoided at all costs.

Living without beliefs – scientific or religious – I do not have to interpret life through the dull light of dogma. Anyone who simply observes the most mundane things of this fantastic existence and marvels at the stunning intelligence that informs it, lives with a sense of aliveness that no dogmas can provide.

The incredible power of the mind leads us to thinking it is the top dog, whereas it is part of a triple power: the trinity of body, mind and spirit. All three are equally important and need to function in harmony. When they do they become the ultimate trinity – not Father, Son and Holy Spirit.

Spirit

Spiritualism is the belief that the spirits of the dead have the ability and the inclination to communicate with the living. It peaked in the nineteenth century with Fox sisters who ultimately confessed that they were cheats. Houdini once attended a séance where it was claimed that a dead spirit played the trumpet. The lights went out and the trumpet did make an uncertain sound, but when the lights came on again the medium had a black ring around her mouth. Houdini had placed boot polish around the mouthpiece of the trumpet when the lights were turned off...

He then offered a vast sum of money to anyone who could prove they had contacted dead people – no one has ever claimed the money. I believe with Shakespeare's Hamlet that death is 'that undiscovered country from whose borne no traveller returns' not even Jesus.

Spirituality is not part of any particular practice, it's much bigger. Spirituality is a certain way of being and includes a sense of connection with something greater. We are divine in the deepest part of our being and don't need any of the 200 gods that men have conjured up out of nowhere.

One of the practical ways our spirit expresses itself is with our intuition. I have had a hearing problem for many years but suddenly there was a buzzing in my head that distorted everything. Neither my doctor nor my audiologist could explain what was happening.

I suddenly felt that the pills I had taken since my triple heart bypass almost 20 years ago were to blame and so I stopped taking them. Within a couple of weeks the distortion disappeared. This episode led me to trusting my intuition much more.

What I did not realise at the time was that there had been a sharp decline in the number of new drugs after the thalidomide disaster. This was one of the darkest episodes in pharmaceutical history. I had just started working as a hearing aid audiologist when a mother asked if I could help her daughter who had hearing problems. However I was shocked when she pulled back her daughter's hair to reveal she had no ears! Sadly I couldn't help, because in those days we needed ears to hang the hearing aids on.

'There has been a fundamental shift in the rationale of drug treatment – we no longer only treat symptoms; we aim to control more aspects of physiology than ever before: blood pressure, glucose level and cholesterol must be brought within "normal" levels in order to reduce the risk of heart attacks and strokes,' writes James Le Fanu in his startling book *Too Many Pills*. It also reveals that doctors are paid by the pharmaceutical companies whenever they prescribe one of their drugs. I find that a totally unacceptable practice.

Our spirit is a powerhouse and equal to the mind. This is not something I believe but something I experienced in the sixties. It is difficult to explain this worldwide Charismatic movement to those who were not involved but I will try.

Only Christians seemed to know about it and they were divided about whether it was of God or the Devil, as usual. It was also linked with the strange biblical phrase 'the baptism of the Spirit' which had only been used by the Pentecostal Church until the 1960s. In fact those of us who were initially involved were called Neo-Pentecostals.

So we decided to meet with their leaders to see if we could unite in some way. After hours of discussion we gave it up as a bad job as they said you **must** speak in tongues to prove you were 'baptised in the Spirit'; we said you **may**. Sadly it proved to be an unbridgeable gap and I began to see dogma as death. Religion turns what happens spontaneously into law.

One of my friends from college popped into my vestry after the evening service and asked me to pray for him to be filled with the Spirit. He had been to the local Pentecostal church who refused to pray for him because he refused to believe their 'tongues as the evidence'. So he came to me and I prayed for him and he immediately spoke in tongues…

In time I came to believe the term being 'filled with the spirit' was also misleading as we were already filled, so I began

Spirituality Should be Divorced from Religion

to pray for people's spirits to be released. On one occasion I prayed for this to happen with four people who came to see me together for help. At the end one person laughed, another cried, the third was silent and the fourth spoke in a language they had never learned.

There is only one thing that is 'the evidence' – your life. As Paul says 'Though I speak with the tongues of men and of angels and have not love, I am become as sounding brass.' Love is the greatest expression of your spirit.

My reason for devoting so much space to this strange Charismatic movement is that some of us are now able to speak in a language we had never learned and I still do. One of my oldest friends asked me if I miss anything from my past experiences. I immediately said 'singing in the spirit', without thinking.

At large gatherings, sometimes with hundreds of people, we gave the audience the chance of expressing themselves in song without any written music and with words they didn't understand. I admit that it sounds like a daft idea but the results were breath-taking. My only regret now is that I will not be able to experience this miracle ever again as I am no longer of part of any religion and never will be.

It is also a demonstration that our spirit is not some vague thing but one third of the trinity that we are. Our problem is that we exalt one of the three attributes above the rest – usually the mind. That is because science has proved so successful in solving many questions we have. It did that by admitting we do not know the answers to the most important questions and I have followed their example.

However, by generally putting the mind in pole position we have devalued our body and our spirit and are not firing on all cylinders now. My reason for devoting so much space to the Charismatic movement is because it enabled those of us involved to speak in a language we had never learned. It is a demonstration that our spirit is not something ethereal but a vital part of the trinity that we are. It also points to the next big event – the coming of Age the Spirit.

George Tarleton

The Journey is the Destination

'The journey is the destination' is a saying that comes from the Orient, where I was born. I dismissed it as one of those sayings they love in the East like 'What is the sound of one hand clapping?' Having lived for over three quarters of a century, I now see its wisdom as my life is a classic example of it.

My destination when I left school was to be an actor. After being converted to Christianity I decided that my destination was to be a preacher and write my own lines. After years of trying to change the church and finding it an impossible task, I quit and became a businessman. Then I became a writer. Now that I have retired from all my labours and had time to reflect, I see clearly that my journey was my destination.

Being rejected by my supposed friends was my salvation. Once I got over my self-pity – which didn't take long – I began to realise that I had been given my get-out-of-jail-free card. Without the imaginary 200 or more gods men have dreamed up (how an earth do you know that you have chosen the right one?) I was now free to live my life without the strange laws that religious people proclaim are God's without any evidence.

Take the first commandment: 'Thou shalt love the Lord thy God with all thy heart, all thy soul, all thy strength and all thy mind.' This leaves no room at all for loving anyone else. Also how can you command someone to love as religion does? As it is impossible to keep this imaginary law, you are forced to confess you sin daily. Guilt is religion's weapon of mass destruction and they use it shamelessly.

The second commandment says we should love our neighbour as ourselves. When we moved to the New Forest, my next-door neighbour was the life and soul of every party we went to but I never really got on with him. This led me to rethink the wisdom of this command which the Bible makes.

When he died his daughter refused to let him be buried next to his wife as he wanted. She had discovered her mother's secret writings which disclosed how her father had treated her mother abominably. So he was buried as far away from her as possible. I have to confess that the only person I have loved as myself is not any of my neighbours but my wife who I have loved for over 60 years.

My move to the New Forest from the concrete jungle of London was a real joy and it changed my view of the countryside. I had thought that people who loved nature were pagans but after a few months I has joined them. I used to walk my dog around Alexandra Palace in London and thought the view was wonderful, but the views in the Forest were not confined to one particular spot but everywhere I looked.

So, with my three different Lassie Collies, we explored the 'New' Forest which will soon be 1000 years old. As I could not express the wonderful beauty of the forest with its deer and great variety of trees, I decided to take up photography. This took some time for me to master it but I'm glad I did as I'm now back in London.

My fear that I was becoming a pagan with my love of nature ceased to matter. The *21st Century Dictionary* says a pagan 'is not a Christian, Jew or Moslem… and without religious beliefs' which is a good enough description of me now. The world's three major religions were all born in the Middle East and are inextricably linked to one another. Judaism was founded in the seventh century BCE, Christianity in the first century CE and Islam in the seventh century CE.

All three Abrahamic religions believe that God revealed himself exclusively to Abraham. Then God tested Abraham's loyalty by demanding that he take his only son Isaac 'whom you love… and sacrifice him as burnt offering.' This must be the weirdest request one father ever made to another and shows they both had needs.

The concept of God being a trinity of Father, Son and Holy Spirit was only finally recognised by the Church in the fourth century and says they are coequal but they are not. The Father is clearly in charge. He sends the Holy Spirit to impregnate the Virgin Mary to give birth Jesus before she is married to Joseph.

Then he sends his sinless son to die for the sins of the whole world which is a strange thing for a loving father to do. If he did that today, Jesus would be taken into care.

After three heart attacks and a triple bypass, I was helped to recover by a wonderful nurse. However there was an inexplicable sadness about her until she discovered I used to be a minister of religion. She then explained that a Christian woman, when she discovered the nurse had a son who had cerebral palsy, said to her 'You must have done something terrible for God to do this to you.' I was so socked that I put my arms around her and said without thinking 'If God did that to you he deserves to burn in Hell for all eternity!' A smile appeared on her face for the first time.

Although I don't believe in Hell or God, I stand by my instinctive response. How can anyone say something like that unless they believe in a vindictive god? The fear of God is not 'the beginning of wisdom' but of ignorance. When you realise that your body, mind and spirit are all equal and allow them to function in unison – you become the ultimate trinity, not God. That is the beginning of wisdom.

I do not want to belong to anything smaller the than the human race which I realise includes the critics who denounce me. 'He drew a circle that shut me out – heretic, rebel, a thing to flout. But love I had the wit to win, we drew a circle that took him in,' wrote Edwin Markham and I wish I had said that.

My Final Word

I ended my last book by saying 'with my track record I would not blame you for thinking I am after gathering another bunch of followers around me. Quite frankly, I have had enough of followers to last me a lifetime! What I am pleading for are seekers.' So I ended with the words of Rainer Maria Rilke: 'I have faith for those things that are yet to be said. I want to set free my most holy feelings. What no one has dared to want will be impossible for me to refuse.'

My last book should have ended with Dr Andrew Walker's quote but arrived too late to be published. As you can see from what he says, I have always been breaking free from the bondage of religion and running toward the light of Life. Life is the greatest teacher because it does not give us all the same old boring advice as religions do. Instead its advice is individually tailored to our changing needs.

As I write this the brave ordinary people of Iran are valiantly challenging the all-encompassing authority of their ayatollahs. They rightly blame their religious leaders for decades of bad economic management, its endemic corruption, its nuclear proliferation, its aggression against its allies, its sponsorship of terrorism and its mindless addiction to the Moslem religion. Protestors now face the death penalty for 'waging war against God!'

Fortunately we are not run by religious zealots in this country. However I suggest we stop propping up the diminishing authority of the Church with our money and give the money to charity instead. Avoid large charities who are part of the charitable-industrial complex, like Oxfam, and go for the smaller, more dedicated ones. I gave my money to one of the well-known large charities until I found out how much of my money was being reinvested in the future of the organisation rather than going to the needy. That may be good business practice but is doesn't help those who need our help and need it now.

George Tarleton

I have come to the conclusion that religion should be ultimately be abolished but realise that is not going to happen any time soon. However religion is beginning to lose its weird grip on humanity and by stopping the flow of money into it we can hasten its demise. This might not seem very revolutionary but, in the world that capitalists have created, money is king and no one can survive without it.

At the source of human awareness lies a silent unchanging and infinite consciousness which has the incredible power to heal ourselves and the world. Our great need is to be totally involved in the present and in rhythm with the vast orchestra of existence which surrounds us. When we do, we become aware that we are living in a grand mystery and become like little children. Returning to innocence with maturity, we become wide-eyed and wise: going about our business as usual but with a twinkle in our eyes.

The present moment is the only one we can really examine and learn from. Driven by the advent of the digital age, which feeds on our capacity to get more and more done in less and less time, we risk never being present with and for ourselves. We never know what is going to happen next because the present moment is the place where all possibilities exist. It is always now, so live here and now, transcending time.

Life is a mystery so awesome that we insulate ourselves from its intensity. To numb our fear of the unknown, we desensitise ourselves to the miracle of living. We perpetuate the nonchalant lie that we know what Life is. Yet behind this preposterous bluff the Mystery remains unchanged, waiting for us to remember to wonder.

The majesty and mystery of the Universe provoke a sense of awe that none of the gods made in our image can match. I simply want people to learn from their own experience of Life as I have learned from mine. One minute I was going about my business as if Life was nothing special. The next I was face to face with the profound, unfathomable breath-taking reality that Life is a mystery.

Spirituality Should be Divorced from Religion

God's greatest moment is when you realise you need no god. Should this statement begin to disturb you, just look up at the cloudless sky at night where you will begin to glimpse a small fraction of the vast Universe that we are part of in all its glory. No manmade god can begin to compete with it.

We now know that our Universe is 13.7 billion years old, 93 billion light years across and filled with 100 billion galaxies, each containing hundreds of billions stars. Without the stars there would be no ingredients to build us for we are made of stardust. Without the Universe's great age there would be no time for the stars to perform their alchemy.

The truth is that the Universe is much bigger than we ever imagined. What we thought of as the Universe is only a mere 4% of something more mysterious scientists call Dark Energy. Then there is Dark Matter that scientists don't have a clue about! So what we think of as space is only a mere 4% of what is there. Then there is 23% is dark energy and 73% is something more mysterious they call Dark Matter...

This is a good place to stop and let you meditate on the mystery we live in and reject the religion's unbelievable answers. The challenge is do you want to live in the cosy comfort of your Christian cage or fly away to the freedom of living in the real world with all its problems and pleasures? Come fly with me.

Postscript

I apologise in advance for not being able to respond to any questions you may have about by experiences which can never change. However learning from Life does not protect us from its pain. My wife has Alzheimer's disease and I look after her 24/7 – it borders on the miraculous that I have managed to write this book which I never planned. In case you think it is God's judgement on her, she has never questioned her Christian faith like me. If it is God's doing then he has hit the wrong target – it should have been me as I would not have remembered enough to write this book!

One way to dismiss my new way of thinking is to claim that I am an atheist. I am not, because I believe we are divine in our deepest identity. Nor am I a theist as I believe that the 200+ gods are manmade and exist only in the minds of their believers. Both theists and atheists offer no proof for their opposite views – just clever words which cancel each other.

Finally I thank my daughter for devoting an amount of her busy life to getting this book published. So I bid you goodbye and trust my words have challenged you to think and **let Life teach you its secrets**.

Yours sincerely

George Tarleton

Lightning Source UK Ltd.
Milton Keynes UK
UKHW010659090619
344071UK00001B/196/P